All Scripture references taken from the KJV of the Holy Bible, unless otherwise indicated.

Devil Weapons: Anger, Unforgiveness & Bitterness

by Dr. Marlene Miles

freshwaterpress9@gmail.com

ISBN: 978-1-960150-27-1

Paperback Version

Copyright 2023

All rights reserved. No part of this book may be reproduced, distributed, or transmitted by any means or in any means including photocopying, recording or other electronic or mechanical methods without prior written permission of the publisher except in the case of brief publications or critical reviews.

Table of Contents

- Foreword 5
- Be Angry, Sin Not 6
- Don't Let the Sun Go Down 8
- Night Watches 11
- Forgiveness 14
- Agree with Your Adversary 20
- The Power to Forgive 22
- Don't Play 25
- Forgiveness Has Power 27
- Frozen 30
- The Night Comes 37
- Power 40
- Powers 44
- Prayer 47
- Use It or Lose It 48
- The Test of Love 54
- Mercy 59
- Devil Weapons 61
- Childhood Vows 63
- Revenge Thinking 68
- How Much Can I Forgive? 70
- Prayer of Forgiveness 76
- Is It Real? 78

Benefits Of Forgiving..80

How Most Curses Work 83

Inflammation..86

Spiritual Things..90

Can Make A Person Sick...90

Benediction 93

Christian books by this author:....................................95

Devil Weapons:
Anger, Unforgiveness & Bitterness

Freshwater Press

USA

Foreword

Nothing in this book is written for you to bop someone over the head with it, telling **them** *what's wrong with them.* This book is to prevent, or correct things in the reader. It is to help *your* prayer life--, both your personal and intercessory prayer life.

The sooner you read this book, the better.

Be Angry, Sin Not

> Be angry, yet do not sin.
> Do not let the sun go down on your anger.
> Ephesians 4:26

If you become angry, do not let your anger lead you into sin and do not stay angry all day. If you become angry, do not sin.

Be angry. Sin not.

We are very fortunate because God has given us Salvation. He's given us the Holy Spirit. He's provided spiritual gifts for us, the Fruit of the Spirit and everything we need for life and for godliness.

We have a great bounty of gifts from God. Have you ever wondered what happens to those gifts if we don't use them? What happens to these gifts from God if we don't access them? Does God just keep them? Are they locked up somewhere to just flow on demand? What if we just don't use them because we don't want to, or we don't know that they exist, or we don't know *how* to use them?

Do these gifts simply evaporate? Do they rot? Do they ruin? Do they just waste away and stink up the place? What happens to them?

This book, **Devil Weapons: Anger, Unforgiveness & Bitterness** which began while praying against the *root of bitterness* will explore all this.

Don't Let the Sun Go Down

Therefore putting away lying… we are members of one another. Be angry and do not sin. Do not let the sun go down on your wrath nor give place to the devil. Let him who stole, steal no longer, but rather let him labor working with his hands. What is good that he may have something to give him who has need. Let no corrupt word proceed out of your mouth. But what is good for necessary edification, that it may impart grace to the hearers. And do not grieve the Holy Spirit of God, by whom you were sealed for the day of redemption.

Let all bitterness, wrath, anger, clamor and evil speaking people away from you with all malice. And be kind to one another, tenderhearted, forgiving one to another, even as God in Christ forgave you.

Therefore, putting away lying, let each one of you speak truth with his neighbor, for we are

members of one another, being angry, and do not let the sun go down on your wrath.

(Ephesians 4:25-32, emphasis added, mine)

What's the big deal about the sun going down on your wrath (anger), is that even a real thing? If any of you have ever had a fever or any kind of ache, haven't you noticed that it seems to get worse when the sun goes down?

Then you know--, yeah, that's a real thing.

Pain may be worse at night because sunshine helps your mood, it is needed to help you make Vitamin D which is needed for proper body function especially regarding muscles, bones and joints. Sometimes warmth helps you feel better, cooler temperatures make you feel worse. So, the sun going down changing how a person may feel is a real thing.

With certain conditions your body position may play a role in how you feel. Standing may be comfortable, sitting, maybe not so much, or vice versa. At night when you lie down things may feel worse. Your body's weight may affect pressure points-, it depends on where your aches are. It depends on what kind of aches they are--, if they are muscular or if it's nerve pain, or joint-related.

If you're by yourself at night for instance, you may be all in your head about how you feel. Sometimes being out and about with people or having friends over is good. Sometimes the distraction is a good thing.

At night your hormone levels, metabolism and everything else that changes to prepare your body for the night and for sleeping may also affect not only how you *feel but how you actually **are***. The anti-inflammatory hormone cortisol that naturally occurs in your body decreases the first half of your sleep cycle to help you sleep. Inflammation really hurts, especially at night. Ouch!

Night Watches

The Bible sets out four periods when the gatekeeper, the watchman (intercessor) must keep watch during the night. There's a first, there's a second, third and a fourth watch of the night. First watch is from 6:00pm to 9:00 pm, the midnight watch is from 9:00pm to midnight. The next watch is from midnight to 3:00am, and then the Dawn Watch is from 3:00 am to 6:00 am.

Why are there night watches? Because things happen at night. Yeah, criminals and whatnot come out at night, but *spiritual* things happen at night, so there should be a *spiritual* watch over your life at night. How do you not know that the physical pain you feel more at night is not related to an increase in negative spiritual activity also happening at night, and you are more sensitive than you think?

Things happen at night, and a lot of things *try* to happen. A lot of evil things go on during the darkness of night. People and other things try to hide under the cover of night.

There you are, sleeping; have you given a thought to a prayer covering for the night? But, there you are, your body and your soul are hanging out in the bed resting, or trying to rest. If your *spirit man* is not built up, while all this flesh and soul resting is going on, you might get into some spiritual situations that you may need God to help you get out of.

Sadly, you might step into a few *spiritual* problems that you won't even know about until way later, because things may not always be immediate. There are things that either go bump in the night or they *try* to go bump in the night. Spiritually there is a lot that we don't know because right now we see through a glass darkly.

Jesus even speaks of His own return. He says He will come like a thief in the night. Yes, thieves are out at night. Why? Well, in the natural, we know what thieves might be trying to take, but spiritually speaking, what could be happening at night?

This book will cover spiritual things, spiritual gifts, and spiritual power--, **especially at night.**

Forgiveness

> But that ye may know that the Son of man hath power on earth to forgive sins, (then saith he to the sick of the palsy (Matthew 9:6 a)

The Son of man has power on Earth to forgive sins. In this verse we know that it is referring to Jesus, but it did not say the Son of God, it said the Son of man. Yes, by Salvation and adoption we aspire to become Sons of God, but are we not also sons and daughters of man? We then may interpolate that we also have the power on Earth to forgive sins. Forgiveness of sins is a power; Scripture leads me to believe that.

So, God puts power on Earth, so we can reach it, man can reach it, and access it. But if we don't use it, if we don't access it what happens to it?

As before stated, what I'm sharing in this book started out while I was praying against the *root of bitterness*. Bitterness spawns from unforgiveness. The Scripture reminds us that Jesus had power on Earth to forgive sins. Jesus is forgiving sins, so if bitterness spawns from unforgiveness, what's our problem? Bitterness should **never** be a problem because we can move in forgiveness, so bitterness never has a chance to even start, much less take *root*.

But man is foolish, stubborn, hard-headed, and not smart sometimes. By not forgiving we are saying we'd rather have bitterness than Jesus.

Jesus, the Son of Man, has power on Earth to forgive sins; so, forgiveness is a power. *What*? Jesus had the power on Earth to forgive sins. That's what the Scripture says, I'm not making it up; it's what it says. So, if we're supposed to be doing what Jesus does--, no, greater things, He said, because He goes to the Father. Then we also have access to this **power to forgive**. We have the power to forgive. Also in the Lord's Prayer we ask God to forgive us *as* we forgive others.

We want forgiveness, but it is contingent on forgiving others. Further, God gives us power to forgive, so really mankind has no excuse.

But if we don't use this power of forgiveness, if we just let it sit there when we could use it, and we refuse to reconcile with our fellow man, or we refuse to play nice, we refuse to be kind, as the verse says--, or we refuse, and we keep refusing, then what happens to this power?

Well, first of all, unforgiveness turns into bitterness which is a resentful *spirit* that refuses to be reconciled. What we have then is bitterness with *power* associated with it.

Don't let the sun go down on your anger. Be angry, but sin not.

Unforgiveness turning into bitterness happened overnight. What happened?

Read on...

I used to think up until last week that what you **did** while angry was the sin. Possibly it is the sin. You might yell, SCREAM, fight, rage, say bad words, key somebody's car, or bash in their head lights. I'm not recommending this to anybody. I thought it's what you *did* while you were angry was the sin.

Perhaps it is. The sin may be your going to sleep *while* you're angry, while you're still in your *flesh*. Maybe that's not even the sin. Perhaps it's both of those things together--, what you do while angry and then top it off, going to sleep while still angry. Or, could it be that the sin is what may happen to your *spirit man* in the night while you're asleep because you went to bed **IN YOUR FLESH**.

Maybe it's all three.

At night, you are in bed. Your soul is slumbering, your flesh is slobbering but your spirit man is still very active. You are asleep and may think you're dreaming, but your *spirit man* is in the spiritual world that never slumbers or sleeps. Your spirit man is interacting--, meeting people and *non-people*--, making deals and covenants while your body sleeps. Yes, your spirit man is interacting with *spirits*, and entities and wickedness in high places and low places – there are witches, wizards, warlocks, astral projected and other human agents of Satan roaming about in spiritual realms seeking what they can steal. They are seeking whom they can kill and or destroy.

Your spirit man is running all of this while your body rests. Sleeps. Dreams. You are out there, man.

Before going to bed, have you built up your *spirit man* today with prayer and the Word? Have you built your *spirit man* up with fasting? Have you built your *spirit man* up with praise, with worship? Have you built your *spirit man* up with **anything**?

Did you pray? Probably not, because you're still mad at Sally Sue.

Did you ask the Lord to forgive you for being in unforgiveness? Probably not; because you think you have a right to not forgive.

So, you go to bed in your flesh while your *spirit man* who has to handle itself, your soul and speak for your flesh for the next 8 hours or so, is **suppressed**.

Is your *spirit man*, strengthened for the night? Probably not. **This could be the sin.** Or it could just be *part* of the sin.

In this spiritual state, are you ripe for the picking by the devil? Possibly. We hope not. But probably, especially if you are still dwelling on the insult or assault that you endured that caused this unforgiveness that you indignantly believe you have the right to harbor.

Apostle Paul would not have told the Christians at Ephesus, and also wrote it down for them and us: *Do not let the sun go down on your anger.*

In plain English, **Don't sleep. Don't try to sleep. Don't go to sleep on unforgiveness.**

Agree with Your Adversary

This Scripture further says to **agree with your adversary quickly.**

The devil is in the details, so once you let the devil in it, *you* become one of the details. If you let the devil get into you, you grieve the Holy Spirit, which the Bible tells us not to do in our Scripture verse of reference.

If you are wondering how the devil got into you because you didn't forgive, well, unforgiveness is not just a choice, it is a *spirit*. It is a *spirit* that is NOT of God. Since it is not of God, guess where it's from? The devil. If you harbor *Unforgiveness* you are harboring a *spirit* from the devil. There you go; you are officially one of the *details* and, not in a good way.

Other things that grieve the Holy Spirit, is abusive language also mentioned in our verse.

Bitterness grieves the Holy Spirit, as does rage and uncontrolled anger. Not having self-control grieves the Holy Spirit. Ignoring the Holy Spirit, especially when He is trying to convict us of sin, also grieves the Spirit.

The Power to Forgive

There you are either sleeping or trying to sleep but having missed this huge *opportunity* to forgive. The devil can send in *unforgiveness* and now it goes into bitterness. The devil can use it. God can't.

If you've not forgiven quickly, you may move into bitterness, which is a work of the flesh, and the devil can use that, but God can't. Because of this, not only have you empowered the devil, but you've also tied God's hands, preventing Him from helping you right now.

If you don't accept God's Word, you are not accepting God; you are rejecting Him. If you don't accept God's gifts, you are also rejecting Him. If you don't use God's **power** as it is to be used, you have rejected Him. If you have not accepted God's help, then you've rejected God.

This is how you've tied God's hand right now, by rejecting Him.

With unforgiveness that has morphed into bitterness, you also have onboard the power that you *should have* used to forgive. It's a power. Did I mention it is a **power**? Unforgiveness sours into bitterness. And now it's bitterness with **power** on it. Not forgiving makes the person who won't forgive feel powerful. That's not by chance; that person has taken the **power** that should have been used for forgiveness and they believe they have appropriated it for themselves, but the demon called unforgiveness has the power now and it uses it to grow, to morph into bitterness, and resentment.

This is a disaster.

You may think you're hurting the person that you won't forgive. If they are sensitive and really care about you, you *may* be hurting them, but it's not as much as you are hurting yourself. Especially if they are matured in Christ, they've probably forgiven you and moved on with their lives. If they are immature and possibly unsaved, you two can wage an epic war on social media or in your neighborhood, that neither of you will win. But you are hurting yourself more than you are hurting them and for more reasons and in more ways than you think.

Read on as we look a little deeper at this. Let's go deeper, *spiritually*.

This is not a small thing. This is a disaster.

By not forgiving and then going to bed angry, you've made yourself a powerful pawn for the devil, and the devil is probably laughing out loud.

Don't Play

You can't play with spiritual things, especially **power**. This is not child's play, and you are not a child. Further, you are accountable for what you choose to do in any situation. Be reminded that you are saved, and you are to agree with the Word of God and do it. It's far too dangerous to play around with unforgiveness, and God's not playing with any of us. Bitterness and unforgiveness has caused feuds, wars and battles, and some of them have lasted a long time, even decades.

But then you know that the son of man has power on Earth to forgive sins, (Matthew 9:6).

We need to pray and ask the Lord to teach us to know the seasons, to know when it's time to forgive someone, to forgive them before it festers into bitterness, because while it's still unforgiveness, here comes the devil. But once it festers into bitterness, the devil latches on and a root of bitterness is begun.

> Reconcile quickly with your adversary. Agree with an adversary quickly while thou aren't with him in the way, (Matthew 5:25).

This verse is about agreeing with your adversary for spiritual reasons, not for your own protection or for the comfort of your flesh. Agree with an adversary quickly, that's what the Word says. When your parent gives you an instruction it requires no further explanation other than, *Because I said so,* you do what your parent says.

God is our Parent.

Do not let the sun go down on your wrath, because God said so.

Yeah, you could be any. The Bible says you can be angry, but sin not. Go ahead. Go through your emotions, go through your *feels*. Feel your *stuff*, but don't stay there.

Forgive each day if you have to, Jesus said it's 70 times seven. Forgive all day long if you have to.

Forgiveness Has Power

Look at this: Jesus forgave a man his sins, and then look what else happened.

> But that you know that the son of man has power on earth to forgive sins. And then he said to the paralytic, arise, take up your bed and go to your house, (Matthew 9:6-7).

Look at that. After Jesus forgave the man, then something favorable happened to the man.

I used to think that the two things that happened in that verse were two separate things.

We see that Jesus, who has the **Power to Forgive**, forgave and at the forgiving of the sin(s) caused the man to be able to get up and walk. Or at least it stopped him from *not* being able to get up and walk. Glory to God.

The question may come to your mind that all those times that people were made well or made whole by Jesus, did He cast out demons? Did He forgive sins? Or did He *heal* them? That question has certainly come to my mind.

The forgiving of sins means the ***iniquity*** associated with having sinned is forgiven. That means the *penalty* of the sin is removed. The penalty being sickness, illness, even death in the case of Jairus' daughter and Lazarus, twice. Bible people understood that if someone was sick that someone had sinned. They had sense enough to know that sin and sin-sickness could be generational. Why don't we seem to know that?

The best answer I have for this from the Holy Spirit right now is that Jesus forgave sins, He forgave the ***iniquity***, which means Jesus FIRED the demons that were *enforcing* the sin covenant. Once they were fired, they had to go because they were trespassing. Once those demons left, THEN the person was healed. Because *with* Jesus and because *of* Jesus, sin doesn't any longer have to be unto death. Sin-sickness is not a terminal disease anymore because of Jesus and with Jesus.

Sickness is under the Curse of the Law. A person breaks the spiritual law, and the penalty is death. Death of something; it could be death of health, or the death of health leading to complete physical death, slowly, over time. It could be death of finances, or opportunities. Jesus, by **forgiveness** of the sin restores a person's soul (emotions) and body. Now instead of sickness, that person is healthy again. Jesus solves the root cause, then the symptoms fall away. Most often, doctors will treat symptoms, but the root cause is still there. The root cause of sickness (and death) is SIN.

Go and sin no more, Jesus said.

Deliverance is the children's bread. Jesus also said that what He did we can do, and even greater things. Therefore, **we** have the power to forgive, we have the power to heal, the power to cast out demons.

Let it be and Amen. Thank You, Lord.

Frozen

When you don't forgive someone, not only does nothing favorable happen, but something ungodly and unfavorable happens. Not only do you fall into bitterness, but you and/or that person may also be **frozen** in place--, frozen in time. And sometimes the person who remains stuck, frozen in place, frozen in *time* is the very one who will not forgive. The other party, who may have a prospered soul, who may have told you the truth in Love, may have moved on with their life. Where you may be the one in the wrong, emotionally wounded, convicted by the Holy Spirit of SIN, but mad at the person who told you the truth in Love, then by so doing, let unforgiveness in.

Oh, the messengers of God. What drama they see.

Maybe by not forgiving, that's exactly what you hoped to accomplish--, to freeze time right there. Your emotions have taken over and your emotions want to **FEEL**. Your emotions want to **freeze** time and *f-e-e-l* in order to *remember* this moment, for survival? So, it remembers, in the attempt to keep this from happening again, because it *feels* so bad? If you sinned, there's nothing to remember except don't sin. If you didn't sin, this is still an opportunity for growth; if the other person is really wrong, forgive them anyway, as led by the Holy Spirit.

This *freezing*, however, is a prehistoric response. Survival mode takes over immediately. Flight fright or **FREEZE** is part of Survival mode. Most who don't forgive think they are wise and are protecting themselves.

Picture the Ice Age squirrel in a mountain of snow looking for a place to bury that acorn to leave it there, forever, to freeze it, to maintain it in that position, forever. He hides it and *freezes* it there to *remember* when he **had** a big, fat, delicious acorn.

Not forgiving is like picking at a scab. You keep picking at it but what's underneath is the same thing that was underneath it yesterday and it has to start all over trying to heal again. You have a boo-boo, an *owie*, God sends a **power** to heal it. That healing power is forgiveness –IF YOU USE THAT POWER, if you use it YOU WILL HEAL.

Forgiveness is healing or beginning the healing--, but you don't want it. Or you only want it temporarily, deciding later on to be angry at that person, and unforgiving all over again.

Forgiveness is a covering that can **heal** an emotional wound. Unforgiveness pulls that "scab" of forgiveness OFF to either see what is underneath, what it looks like today, or to start the pain all over again. You **have to** often pull the scab off if you've made a deal with the devil that you will NEVER forgive So and So. You HAVE TO, you MUST PULL THAT SCAB OFF AGAIN SO YOU CAN FEEL THE HURT AGAIN TO REMIND YOURSELF TO NEVER FORGIVE SO AND SO.

Some people want to keep feeling the pain, it places them at the center of a drama and makes them feel important. This is all a devil trick; don't fall for it.

In unforgiveness, you believe you've frozen time with your powerful self. You've used the POWER to Forgive to freeze time instead. Really? Yes. Really, for yourself... that's the only person you've really affected, unless the person you're mad at lives or works with you, and you are going to PICK the fight all over again every day. Like picking at a scab.

Chances are very high that they've moved on and forgotten it. You do know that they interact with other people other than you? You are not their entire focus, so why make them yours? Additionally, there are other people that you need to interact with and not this one person that you've made into a whole idol.

When you've forgiven but the other person hasn't, resentment, bitterness, revenge, vengeance, WITCHCRAFT is the usual result. Sometimes it's **both** of you, but most of the time it's the *one* who won't forgive is driving things to the negative. Worse than that, the unforgiving person empowers the devil by involving the devil. Whatever you do in the Earth that involves *spiritual* power will come from one of two sources-- God? Yes please.

The devil--, no thank you, devil power most often involves witchcraft.

You could fall under judgment with God for not forgiving another saint when you should have, for harboring resentment, for refusing to be reconciled, for planning revenge, and for staying in your flesh.

NOT forgiving when you have the **POWER to forgive** is worse than you think it is. In the Old Testament, Job didn't get deliverance until he prayed for his friends. In the New Testament, Jesus said that neither the man nor his parents had sinned, but this was to the Glory of God. Jesus had the power to forgive and knew it. Job had been operating under the premise that he didn't have the power to forgive by sending up offerings for all of his 10 children every week. However, when his friends (and wife) advised him incorrectly, he could have moved into offense with them. Had he, he wouldn't have prayed for them, and it is when he prayed for others, Job's evil and unfortunate conditions immediately reversed.

Sometimes GOD has set you up to be blessed by *praying for another*; sometimes the same power that delivers another will deliver YOU. Look at JOB.

Further, what the devil means for your harm, God can turn it to your good. The devil sends someone *to* insult you, hurt or assault you in some way to lead you into unforgiveness and bitterness. The devil pretty much knows that you will jump into your flesh, so here we go!

But GOD turns that incident into an opportunity for you to be BLESSED. Because you don't fall into the devil trap of unforgiveness; you instead forgive THEM AND PRAY FOR THEM. Pray for those (saints) that despitefully use you.

In no way when dealing with unrepentant people, bent on stealing, killing and destroying do you give them the chance to kill you or mess with your purpose, ministry, spouse, or destiny. The Book of Luke talks about coats and cloaks--, that is *things*, but not life, health, virtue, or family.

Pray for the ones that God says to pray for and the ones that God *allows* you to pray for.

But pray.

If you are not prayerful you won't know who you are dealing with. If God doesn't want you to pray for someone, HE will tell you, don't you just decide on your own, especially because of unforgiveness toward them.

Last year God clearly told me regarding two different people that I know, by saying that they have rejected Him. Period. That's it.

The Night Comes

Things happen at night. Build up your *spirit man* while it is day, because the night comes when you can't do that work because you are resting your soul, you are slumbering and slobbering, as I said.

That Scripture indicates that Jesus expects us to really know what time it is--, when it's time to pray. A little folding of the hands, a little sleep – *spiritual poverty* may come upon you. You may close your eyes for a moment, and then the moment's gone. You have to discern the time, so you don't miss *your* time, your season. Your destiny moment could have been in one of the moments that you FROZE in unforgiveness, with your powerful self.

Or it seems like maybe only paused for a moment, but years went by, decades went by. So much time has gone by that you may have *missed your season*, your season(s), or your *times while being stuck*. Sadly, you're the one who chose to be stuck, you and unforgiveness, with or without bitterness and resentment.

Oh Lord, I pray that you redeem the time for us.

You just closed your eyes for a moment, it seemed, while you wallowed in your self-justified unforgiveness and bitterness, but so much time has passed by. It's like watching a movie late at night, you close your eyes for a few moments, then you wake up and the TV's watching you. The whole movie is over.

If the movie was your Destiny, you missed it.

So don't let time, as in seasons pass you by. It only takes a moment because the devil is waiting for you to fall. He's been waiting for you to fall into unforgiveness. He's waiting for you to fall into the flesh. He's waiting. He doesn't sleep, but you have to; we are humans. We have to.

The devil has lots of tactics, many of them happen *at night*, overnight, while you're still festering over your *previous* best friend, waiting for him or her to come to *you* and apologize to *you*. Instead, apologize and forgive and move on with life, move forward in life.

Time is one of your most valuable resources. Our times are in God's hands, but so is Power. Power belongs to God. Divine, spiritual, God-given power that God has put here in the Earth, *near you, in you,* that you can access. We all can. It's in you. It's near you, the Devil knows that too, so don't let it fall to the ground like crumbs from the table.

Power

Being saved, we all are anointed, we all have power, and we have access to power. If we pray, we have access to *much* power. When an assault happens to you, God gives you the authority and the *power* to handle the situations that you find yourself in. Do you abuse that God-given power, or do you *use it* as God has instructed already in His Word?

That's why the power is so close, even *in* you so you can have access to handle this situation **yourself** instead of calling on God for things that you should and could be handling **yourself**. The anointing IS the Holy Spirit. As we grow in the LORD, we **grow in grace**…just as a child would grow, you give them more and more authority, autonomy, power, money, grace; God is doing that for us.

If a spiritual crumb falls from your table, spiritual hellhounds are waiting. They are waiting for any crumb of power, authority, grace that you misuse, let drop, fall, or let sit around unprotected, unnoticed, unused, —the power that God provides that you miss. Forgiveness has power with it and Grace is also a power. You are a powerful being walking around here, don't behave as if you have no power. If you are a *king,* is it becoming to behave as a commoner? Jesus is King of kings; the *little k* kings are us. We need to conduct ourselves according to who we are and whose we are. Unforgiveness, tantrums and pity parties are not becoming a king, even a *little k* king.

Worse, if you misuse power, it will always invite and most often will include the devil. Misused Godly power ignites the anger of God, it creates evil covenants, soul ties and/or witchcraft.

If you, yourself were a money tree, with money hanging off every limb, and since money is power, you'd know that you had power then, right? Will you let that money fall to the ground or just blow away and not use it? Won't you know how much money is on your tree and where it is located on your tree?

Will you not know HOW that money came to be and if you will get more, or if this is it? Or is this *it* for today? Once you run out you have to wait until tomorrow or another SEASON to get more. So now, without it will you suffer? Will you let people just come and take it? Will you let evil people take it? Worse, take it and use it ***against*** you? Of course, not.

Will you just hand money (power) to them? When you don't use the power of forgiveness for forgiveness you are handing over power to evil. You can know because bitterness is an escalation from forgiveness. When a problem gets worse, instead of better or fully resolved you can know the devil is in it.

Anything that you let fall from your money tree will hit the ground where evil scavengers are waiting for it.

Do you just think the devil's messing with you for fun and games? Maybe he's petty like that, but in reality, you've got something, some things that he wants. He wants your soul. He wants to either shatter or break your spirit so you can't have communion with God. Without communion with God, the devil owns you.

Lucifer got kicked out of Heaven because he wanted God's worship. He wanted God's place. He wanted God's power. God entrusts **you** with power, even the ***power to forgive***, not to forgive all man's sins unto Salvation, but you have the power to forgive offenses and to forgive one another.

When you decide or choose not to use the power that God has entrusted to you, leaving that POWER unprotected, unguarded (by prayer), just lying on the nightstand while you go to sleep. Oh, God help us all.

> For the word of the cross is folly to those who are perishing, but to us who are being saved, it is the power of God. God's power is it's for salvation.
>
> 1 Corinthians 1:18

The devil doesn't forgive. Don't be like the devil.

Power*s*

God gives us all kinds of power. He entrusts us with power. Power to be a witness. The power to testify. Power to prophesy. Power to forgive. The power of Grace. Yes, Grace is a power. The power of faith, the power of Mercy. And He gives us the power gifts of the Holy Spirit, the Gifts of special faith, gifts of healing, and the working of miracles. Include with that, the power to get wealth. All of these are powers that God entrusts to us. This may not be comprehensive list because God is gracious, provident, abundant and generous.

No matter what the power, if we don't use them or use them in *season* and use them appropriately, they could be abused, misused, misappropriated, stolen, or lost. Sometimes, many times, reversed and used against us.

If a small child has anything of value, any bully can take it from him. If a spiritual child has

POWER, the devil will be waiting like a bully to TAKE it from you.

> As for me, I'm filled with power. With the spirit of the Lord, and with justice and might to declare to Jacob his transgression, and to Israel his sin. Micah 3:8

Remember Saul turned into another person, because he was in the company of the Prophets. **God gives us power**. Sometimes the power is for us, sometimes it's for others, sometimes it's for both.

When we don't use the power that God has given us to use, in the way God says, it usually gets perverted and used to work *against u*s. A person with a gift of prophecy may not even know what it is and may listen to the world tell him that he is "psychic." Yes, he can hear spiritually, but being psychic and prophetic are two entirely different things. One is a great grace from God and the other will lead to misinformation and misleading self and others into disaster.

The power to get wealth is another power that if it not used *in season* and properly, it tends to the opposite, poverty.

Tithing, for example, and giving gifts teaches obedience, yes, but it also teaches us to know and observe *seasons*. If we know the harvest season that means we must know the planting and the cultivating seasons. We will be aware of seasons. We'll know when seasons change. We won't just look at the sky to see if it's red and what the weather will be tomorrow. We'll know the full *climate—the natural and the spiritual climate of* what's happening. We'll know what seasons are upon us. God is always teaching us the rhythm of life.

Prayer

Lord, teach me to know the seasons and discern the times. Teach me to know when to do what in my life, in the life of my family, and in the life of others, so that Your hand of blessing is always on us, that Your face is turned toward us.

Father, forgive us and give us another opportunity that we don't waste, and help us that we do not pervert any of the gifts or any of the powers that You've given us. That You would be glorified, and that we be trusted in Jesus' Name.

Use It or Lose It

Some of the power that God has given us access to is *for* us, and some of that power is for others. Either way, ultimately, we have to *use* power the way God says to use it. We have to know that power is available to us. We have to **know how** to use it, and we need to protect it by not being careless or frivolous.

Power protects us. But we also protect it by possessing our souls, by building up our *spirit man,* using power properly, and by staying out of the flesh. Because if we don't use the power that God has for us, the way we should, it becomes polluted, perverted, and it may be stolen and misused or even used against us by the enemies of God, who are our enemies too.

When we don't use the power of forgiveness, for instance, it turns into bitterness. If we don't use the power of love, to love, it turns into fear. God can't use fear, but He can use love.

The devil can't use love, but he can use fear and use it against you.

You see, the very thing that God intends the power to be used *for* is the protection to keep the enemy away from it. God is clever like that.

You may be wondering, why is your life looking the opposite of what you think it should be? Are you using the power that God entrusted to you in the way that God wants you to use it? Are you forgiving people? Are you using the power of forgiveness? Or are you letting it fester into bitterness? Are you using the ***power*** of love? Are you loving people anyway, no matter what they do to you, no matter what kind of people they are? Are you loving them with the *agape* love of Christ?

Are you letting it turn into fear or hatred? Are we paying less time knowing the seasons, knowing the times, and knowing when and how to use spiritual Gifts, or how to use the Fruit of the Spirit. It's critical to know when to use it and how to use it. Just as in the natural, there's a timing for everything.

Unforgiveness ferments into bitterness if we don't forgive.

In relationships, there's the timing for things. Have you ever noticed that in a relationship there's a certain time that you tell the person you're dating that you *love* them? If you don't tell them at the right time, after a while you may become afraid to tell them, or they may be afraid to tell you for both or either of you afraid of rejection. The relationship may go into the Friend Zone or break up completely as you watch the one you wanted become interested in someone who will say, *I love you* to them.

Oh, silence can be so loud sometimes, can't it?

Love not used, turns into fear. Then that can turn into rejection instead of acceptance. It's an opposites game.

If we don't use the gift of faith that God has given us, it turns into doubt. God can't use doubt, but the devil can. The devil can't use your faith in God, but he can use doubt and use it against you.

When it's *pure* power that's when God can use it, but when man **pollutes** power with flesh and evil, evil intent, evil emotions, and an evil heart, it becomes a devil deal.

Beware of the leavening of the Pharisees. Hypocrites say they forgive, but they don't. Like two kids who are made by their parents to say, *Sorry*, but neither one of them mean it, so both kids are hypocrites, like little baby pharisees. God can't use that. Fake sorry's have the devil in them. Once the devil gets in it, God's not.

God's not messing with any that or any of us.

The devil is not stronger than God, but once a person has allowed himself to be polluted and defiled in a devil deal, God is not dealing with it.

But with God, every morning there are new mercies.

When we don't use the gift(s) that God has given us, that He has appropriated and made available to us in the right season, at the right time. ***The devil can get in the details***. That's how the devil can either usurp that power or keep you from using it.

The devil knows this. If this happens, then we've got to fall on our face, on our knees, and ask God to fix the problem *we* created because we didn't use what He had given us, or we didn't use it properly.

We must repent for our disobedience and for *dissing* God. We need to recognize God, recognize the gifts, recognize the power, and recognize the seasons, the time, and the times. The time to forgive is always now. Right now! With a quickness, while you are in the moment with the person who offended you.

Do not let the sun go down on your anger. Do your work while it's day, for the night comes when no man can work. If we don't forgive, sooner or later we may have to ask God for a do over. We may have to ask God to redeem the time, for more reasons than unforgiveness, but still unforgiveness is a huge usurper of power and a time waster. We may have to ask Him to restore the years, and we can go boldly, we can ask God to let us do this all over again, but should we *have* to?

In our repentance, we must promise to use the power of forgiveness and use it appropriately and not make this error again. We have to renounce every evil, devil contract, every evil covenant, every soul tie we made by declaring that we would not forgive in the first place. Promise God that we won't do that again.

We can grow more each day in discerning seasons and *times* by first knowing that the fear of the Lord is the beginning of Wisdom and knowledge. We should practice the fear of the Lord. We should also grow in the Fruits of the Spirit.

We should be led by the Spirit. We should be led by the direct prompting of the Holy Spirit of God. We need to be able to hear God, know His voice, and be obedient to Him, because just hearing His voice but not doing anything is still disobedience.

Anger is a devil trick that blocks blessings from coming to you. If the devil can get you into anger, you will repel wealth, health, joy, peace and all other blessings of God like the Plague.

The Test of Love

So, there's a *spirit of power* and there's self-control. Another very important thing is God's test of love. God's test of love is rigorous because the power gifts work by love. We have to love our enemies, that is, with the *agape* love of Christ.

Love keeps us out of our flesh.

How is that?

If we're loving people, there's no way we can go into hatred, heresies, division or any of the work of the flesh. We can't do it. They're opposed to each other, and Love is stronger, so it will prevail.

And the test of love seems to be about emotions, forgiveness, and material things. These are the very things that hinder love. These are the things that test a man. These are exactly the things that Jesus had to be tested on. It's an open book test, if you'll just open your Bible you can pass it like Jesus did. There are many Bible translations now so that you can choose one that you understand well and then allow the Holy Spirit to teach you the *Spirit* of those words on the pages of the Bible.

These tests are the things that Jesus endured. Love your enemies; Jesus did.

People wanted what they could get from Jesus-, just like you, right? But if they couldn't get what they wanted from Jesus, whatever that was, then they hated Him. Sound familiar? Marvel not; they hated Jesus first. Jesus had to love the people who hated Him--, the Pharisees and Sadducees, the Sanhedrin Council, and the Romans. That was a lot of hate coming at Jesus. Yet Jesus prayed for the Multitude, and these people were all part of the Multitude.

The Bible says to love your enemies, do good to those who hate you. Because if you hate, you are indicating that you have fear, and if you have hate, you're in fear. You should not fear what man can do to you. We've not had to go through anything like what Jesus had to endure, but He remained fearless even in all He had to go through because He still had love.

Bless those who curse you. Jesus was cursed at, spit on and abused. Pray for those who mistreat you. These are all tests of love. You can pray for the salvation of unrepentant sinners who may be trying to kill you, but do not pray that they be empowered to destroy you.

Being mocked, cursed, or abused are times when you can easily go into the flesh. But Jesus didn't.

Jesus prayed for everyone. He forgave them, He said. **Father, forgive them. They don't know what they do.** As bad as He was being treated, He didn't go into the flesh. We need to strengthen our *spirit man,* so we also don't go into the flesh or go easily into the flesh and that if we fall, if we become angry, we come out of the flesh quickly, that is, we sin not.

If somebody slaps you on one cheek, turn the other one. If somebody takes your coat, don't withhold your cloak from him. Give Him that too. They took Jesus's coat and His robe. Back in those days what you wore said who you were, so they were trying to strip Him of identity. When people take things from you, they want your *stuff*. It should be easy for us to not go into the flesh over that, unless we are overly fond of our stuff--, which is idolatry. There are identity thieves out there, but for the most part thieves want *stuff*.

Give to everyone who asks you. If anyone takes what belongs to you, do not demand it back. I didn't see in my Bible where anyone asked Jesus for anything that He didn't give them. Any sinner or seeking person who asked Jesus for anything that He had that He could give, He gave. I don't think He ever refused anyone who asked. I didn't see that. Not once.

The blessings of God are yea, and amen; Jesus treated everyone as God would have treated them. They got love, kindness and Grace. God rains on the just and the unjust alike. These are all tests of love, and if you love those who love you, what credit is that to you? Yeah, what's a quid pro quo, right? God is not transactional; He doesn't do something because He will get something back from you later. God is relational.

Even sinners love those who love them--, (their version of love anyway). Do good to those who love you. Even sinners can do that. If you lend to those to whom you expect repayment, what credit is that to you? Even sinners lend expecting to be repaid in full.

I have a question: If you only lend. When do you give? God loves a cheerful giver. I didn't see any mention in my Bible about a cheerful lender. When do you *give* if you only lend expecting it back?

Love your enemies, do good to them and lend to them without expecting to get anything back. Then your reward will be great, and you will be children of the Most High. Because God, is kind to the ungrateful and the wicked.

The Ministry of Jesus Christ is to the ungrateful and the wicked, after all. The Ministry of Jesus Christ is to the Multitude. Before Salvation we were in that Multitude. He pulled us out of the Multitude. That's where He found us in our sin and in our polluted blood, defiled and in our sin sickness. He was gracious, kind and merciful. To us, the ungrateful and the wicked. How dare we not pay it forward or extend the same or perform ministry as we've been instructed?

Mercy

The Scripture further says be merciful just as your Father is merciful. This test of mercy is a test of our similitude to our Father. Power works by love. So can one have or be filled with the Holy Spirit but not have love or not have *enough* love, so the gifts don't work.

Unforgiveness shows a lack of love.

What is the immeasurable greatness of his power toward us who believe according to the working of his great might? (Ephesians 1:19).

God is powerful, merciful, kind, and He trusts us. God is light, the bright ad Morning Star, and that is power. All power belongs to God. God is the source of Wisdom. He's the source of knowledge. He's the source of Truth and Light.

In Genesis, God created light three days before He created the Sun, the moon, or the stars. Think on that. God created light three whole days before He created the Sun, the moon and the stars. This makes it abundantly clear that **power belongs to God.**

> They will not need the light of a lamp or the light of the sun, for the Lord God will give them light. Revelations 22:5

He gives us power. God graciously supplies us power to do wonders in the Earth, not to ignore, not to reject, not to play with, not to hand over to or lose to the devil while we're trying to win a feud against a friend or a former friend. This is why we don't lean to our own understanding, because it's stupid to do that. I've said it before, but humans would have no idea, when enacting revenge, *how much* payback is enough payback. Man would have the tendency to go overboard. But God's power is mighty, His Wisdom is deep, and His judgements are balanced. All that is for a victory in our witness and our testimony. All to God's glory. Amen.

Forgiveness is a test of Love. Forgiveness is a power, and it is a gift from God because it is much easier to forgive than to uproot a *root of bitterness*.

Devil Weapons

Unforgiveness and bitterness are devil weapons. Recall our foundational Scripture verse:

> Be angry, yet do not sin. Let not the sun go down on your anger, (Ephesians 4:26).

If you become angry, do not let your anger lead you into sin. Do not stay angry all day. Be angry but DO NOT SIN.

Anger follows frustration and disappointment, and injustices. We risk sin when anger becomes unhealthy. Anger becomes unhealthy when it overstays and lasts a long time. At that time, it becomes chronic anger when it moves into unforgiveness and bitterness. Then a *root of bitterness* is established. Sometimes you hear it called a *seed of bitterness*, but once a seed germinates it becomes a *root of bitterness* and you know it has lasted too long if it has taken root.

The Bible says it lasts too long when it lasts more than a **day**. Have you ever tried to root a plant cutting? It takes a while to root, more than a day, sometimes about a week or two.

God has a different timing that we are to acknowledge, concerning forgiving one another, according to the Bible, **you've got until the sun goes down to get past this, to work through it, and to get past it.** Unforgiveness feeds chronic anger and leads to bitterness.

Childhood Vows

Do you remember as a child being upset or angry? Maybe you weren't a spoiled child, but you were childish, or thinking that you weren't getting your way. You may have been thinking, *I don't like this*, escalating to more childish thoughts such as *I'll show them. What if something happens to me? They'll be sorry then*. You may have had other childish plans in your head about making people feel bad because you felt bad.

Those childish childhood vows were signs that you did not have a forgiving spirit, and you were not a forgiving child. Did you grow out of that, or are you still an unforgiving, rigid, unyielding person?

We all know the verse, *No weapon formed against me shall prosper*. What if **you** formed the weapon, or helped form the weapon, beginning years ago? Decades ago--, with your childish emotions, moods, thoughts, and mouth? And, with the help of the devil. After all, you were unsaved then.

As a child, the thoughts in your head could range anywhere from planning to run away from home to the absolute worst. Maybe you didn't have a happy childhood home. Or maybe you just didn't have your way. I pray that the Lord will heal you from that, in Jesus' Name.

When you think about it, desiring or being willing to be hurt yourself to enact a punishment or revenge on someone else is pretty dire. It's really far-fetched--, over emotional and childish. It may have been the most childish thing, or the most desperate or most ungodly thing you've ever thought of.

But you were a child.

If no one ever corrected you, let me do that today. Let me do it now.

You do **not** want something bad to happen to you.

You do **not** wish anything bad would happen to you.

You do **not** want to use yourself, your body, or any part of yourself or your life to punish others.

You do **not** really want to punish anyone.

Revenge belongs to the Lord, so you don't have to plan revenge or sacrifice any body parts, run away, or get lost in a forest to hurt other people unless you are a child, and you still think like a child.

This Scripture says, *When I was a child I thought like a child.* But now that it says I'm a man--, well, a grown person, *so I've put away childish things.*

When you were a child, maybe then you did think as a child, but not now. It is your obligation, and duty, to put away childish thinking, childish speaking, and to guard your words and guard your thoughts.

Because childish words, childish vows, childish thoughts were done in ignorance, but in so doing, you may have invited the devil. Yes, even then. You could have invited evil into your vow. Let's take a moment and pray about that right now.

Father, Lord, in the Name of Jesus, I ask for Your forgiveness for evil words spoken, vows made, oaths created in my childhood when I wasn't even of age to fully understand what I was saying. I plead the Blood of Jesus over those words, over ungodly oaths.

I repent of plotting revenge or holding on to hurts and anger, needlessly. Father, I repent of making ungodly childhood vows, and I renounce them now, in the Name of Jesus.

In addition, I now renounce all other *never* and *always* vows that I may have spoken as a child regarding my adulthood.

Father, please **heal** my inner child, so that I can be made whole emotionally, mentally, physically, and spiritually. Restore my soul, in the Name of Jesus.

I ask You to allow me the freedom in You, Father, to be the me that you intended for me to be from my birth before negative and foolish vows were ever spoken.

I forgive myself for making childish vows, and I believe that by the Blood of Jesus, I am forgiven. Release me from every curse, responsibility, liability and iniquity of speaking evil words over my future life.

Father, I do not want anything negative, ungodly or anything unhealthy to happen to me or to anybody else. I don't want anyone else to feel hurt or be hurt because of me or because I hurt.

Lord, I break every curse that has come from these vows or oaths. I break the power of every evil force that was released to enforce these curses over me, my family, my destiny, future, ministry, and purpose.

Thank You, Lord, that my family and I are covered by the Blood of Jesus, Who has redeemed us from every curse of the Law. Lord, by Your Holy Spirit, please reverse all the damage done by childish curses that I spoke over my own life.

I pray that they will never return to me or hinder my life again or my family's life again. In the Name of Jesus, I pray Amen.

Revenge Thinking

That childish thinking was revenge thinking. As a child when you felt hurt, you wanted the person (people) who hurt you to also feel hurt and *emotional* pain. Now, as an adult we should be thinking differently. We should be thinking about forgiveness and how to maintain relationships, not to end them. Not to separate ourselves from them or run away from them or anything else more drastic.

We should work to maintain relationships with people, even people who may sometimes disagree with us because God does. God wants to keep people; He is relational. People may hurt our feelings from time to time, or we may be disappointed by them or with them. We shouldn't want to get back at them or hurt them, but instead we need to move in forgiveness.

We don't want to constantly think on past hurts. Instead, we want to think on ***these things*** and the peace of God which passes all understanding will guard your hearts and minds in Christ Jesus.

> Finally, brothers, whatever is true, whatever is honorable, whatever is right, whatever is pure, whatever is lovely. Whatever is admirable, if anything is excellent or praiseworthy, think on those things. (Philippians 4:8)

We are called to forgive. We are supposed to forgive. The Bible says that we can be angry, we can go through our emotions, go through our paces, but don't sin and don't let the sun go down on our wrath.

We are to be tenderhearted one to another and kind, forgiving one another even as God in Christ forgave you, (Ephesians 4:32).

How Much Can I Forgive?

Now we get to the crux of this message. *How **much** can you forgive*? If you know you've reached the limit of how much you can forgive, what's next? But people you know are still acting the same over and again, requiring you to do all the forgiving while they just do as they please. Sometimes people don't change, so you're going through the same paces over and over again.

How much you can or do forgive depends on your relationship with God, how submitted you are to the Holy Spirit and your soul's prosperity.

Unforgiveness leads to resentment and bitterness, and all this can lead to real sickness in the body as in chronic unforgiveness. You have to put your negative thoughts and emotions away, because if you keep rehearsing them over and over again, you might convince your body that this thing is happening all over again every day. So, every time you think about it, your body goes through all of that stress all over again. Your body is not designed for that. You cannot handle that. Nobody can.

Or worse, you might be the type who adds up all of the hurts of your life together into one big ball of confusion. You may remember and add up all the wrong stuff done to you and rehearse it over and over to the max to anybody who will listen.

Don't do that.

Not to scare anyone, but among other things, cancer absolutely has emotional roots. Medical evidence suggests that repressed anger, repressed hate and resentment play a crucial role in the development of diseases in the body, including cancer.

When you rehearse hurts and wrongs done over and over, stress hormones are released in the body by emotional triggers, which puts you into *survival mode*. These things suppress the immune system and MAY LEAD TO a stress overload, which may lead to sickness, disease, and even cancer.

We plead the Blood of Jesus, but we need to know that sustained levels of stress hormones jump you right into survival mode.

I think this is one of the number one reasons why you should not ever manipulate a relationship. You shouldn't try to manipulate your life, the lives of the people you know or the people that you want in your life. We shouldn't rely on our own understanding, but we need to acknowledge God and incline our ear to God, to hear where He wants us to go, what He wants us to do, who He wants us to be with, and who we're supposed to be with. God knows who we should be connected to and married to, because that's a long-term, forever commitment.

So, we don't force our way into relationships. We don't force people or trick people into being in relationship with us, because this could end up being the most stressful thing you ever do. We see what stress can do to the body, to the mind, and what it can do over the long term.

It may also end up being one of the most hurtful relationships you could ever have. If it's forced, it's not real if God's not in it.

A fake, manipulated life--, who wants that, no matter how good it looks on the outside, no matter how good it looks on Facebook? Nobody wants a fake, manipulated life and a controlled marriage, that could be completely against the will of God. If this is the case, *at least* those two people would completely miss their destinies.

If you're praying about it--I don't know who you're praying to, but if it's not of God, then who are you praying to? That entity could bring what you're praying for to you. Once you receive that something that you shouldn't even be praying for, then you're really going to be sorry.

You can't manipulate a life. You can't set it up, you can't fake it because it will take too much manipulation to maintain it. It's going to take too much of you and your time to manage it every day. There's your stress right there--, constant stress.

Even if your spouse is faithful and coming home at night, it might look good on the outside. The reality may be that there's stress, bickering and arguments because you're constantly in the flesh trying to maintain, excuse me, manipulate and control someone else's life.

That's not what God intended. Jesus came that we may have life and have it more abundantly, (John 10:10b). Life in the flesh is full of resistance. Life in the *Spirit* brings peace and fullness of joy in the Holy Ghost. Jesus and our relationship with Him, and a prayer life, a good strong prayer life, walking in the Spirit takes us out of survival mode. It removes those stress hormones; it brings us relief from all the stresses, and it brings us Peace.

People who *pretend* in relationships, suppressing their emotions, women especially, are more likely to show changes in stress hormones that can contribute to diseases such as cancer, or not surviving cancer. I'm not trying to depress anybody; I'm just trying to inform you.

Suppression of anger was the most common trait among people with breast cancer. Resentment tears down the immune system, and is a form of anger. It tears it down and it causes an increase in the risk of a heart attack, cancer and diabetes. Knowing that resentment is a form of anger confirms that that anger was slept on, implanted, allowed to take root, nurtured and allowed to grow up, to form a horrible weapon that the devil could attack you with.

Forgiveness is the solution to anger, bitterness, and resentment.

All this information I'm sharing is prominent research from studies from prominent universities in the United States such as Stanford, Duke, and VCU.

There's even a study that says that people with chronic back pain suffer less pain if they *forgive* others versus holding on to unforgiveness.

Chronic unforgiveness causes stress. Period.

Forgive yourself and others.

Prayer of Forgiveness
(For self or others)

Father, thank You for Your love, for the Grace You freely offer. Help me to stop focusing on myself and how I feel, what I want and what I need. Lord help me to use the *power of forgiveness* that You have graciously given to us, just as Jesus had the power on Earth to forgive sins. I know that I do not have the level of forgiveness power to Salvation, but help me offer my forgiveness to those who've injured, hurt, disappointed or embarrassed me.

I set aside all selfishness, entitlement, pettiness, pride and feelings of revenge, and I offer agape love and forgiveness to all who I feel have wronged me in the past. By Your Holy Spirit, Lord help me release them all.

Lord, break every evil covenant made from unforgiveness, bind every devil assigned to enforce every evil covenant and soul tie. Release me from all iniquity and into Your Love. Thank

You for Your Grace and Mercy, in the Name of Jesus, Amen.

Is It Real?

Repeatedly rehearsing the negative moments of your life confuses your mind. Is it real or is it Memorex—is it a recording? Every time a person thinks of their transgressor, their body has a negative response. If you're the type who remembers every word as if it was yesterday, you are flooding stress hormones, like a poison into your body on a regular basis.

You need to change the way you think. Instead, to get over these negative events and memories, think on *these* things--, things that have good report and have virtue, things that have value, things that are Godly. Don't keep rehearsing past hurts.

Unfreeze your thought life. Nothing changes by rehearsing the past. By not forgiving and repeatedly thinking on hurts, you abuse the *power* that should be used for forgiveness on the hurt, to make it worse. Every time you replay the event and think about what you wish you had said, or what you wish you had done instead of what you did, you are again not forgiving, and you are freezing the trauma. Don't do that.

God can heal all the broken hearts, He can heal all the sick, He can heal any disease. God can heal all unhealed hearts, all unresolved, issues, all unmet needs, and all painful memories from childhood and beyond. **You** just have to make yourself stop thinking on negative things. You have to practice thinking on things that are lovely, true, have a good report and have any virtue.

Prayer takes us out of survival mode, brings us to a place of calm, and peace, and healing. To counter a negative thought, you have to speak the opposite of it 10 times. Might as well do that in prayer.

After prayer, do something; take action. Do something different than what you've always done. Make new memories. Make new friends. Take a walk. Get some new activities, new hobbies. Do something different.

Benefits Of Forgiving

Be angry; sin not.

Jesus has the power to forgive. So, we surmise there must be *power in forgiveness*. There are amazing benefits for you in forgiving others.

When Jesus forgave the paralytic man, Jesus told the man to get up, take up your bed and go home. For everyone who is frozen in unforgiveness, you must change from choosing to not forgive to *choosing* **to** forgive. You must choose to release bitterness and all of its roots. You must choose to let go of resentment and take up your bed, **unfreeze** yourself, **unfreeze** your life and go home or go somewhere. You don't have to go home, but just get out of that place where you're stuck. Take up your bed and live. Walk. Go. Be. Do.

Forgiving others has **power** with it, and it can resurrect things. It can resurrect relationships. Releasing grudges and bitterness leads to improved health and peace of mind.

Forgiveness may also redeem the relationship that you're really upset about in the first place. Forgiving, having a kinder, gentler, *forgiving spirit* means that you have developed in the Fruit of the Spirit. Overall, this will lead to better relationships with others. You'll be more pleasant to be around because you're not dragging emotional and spiritual baggage everywhere you go.

Unforgiveness takes you into survival mode where stress hormones are running wild and rampant in your body, making you anxious, giving you high blood pressure, making you depressed. Your immune system is suppressed when you're in survival mode.

You get healthier when you forgive because your immune system, heart health, and your digestive health all improve. You might even stop grinding your teeth. Forgiving others generally improves your sense of well-being.

All body systems are affected in unforgiveness. Can't you see now how badly you're hurting yourself by not forgiving that person that you may have vowed to never forgive?

Yeah, someone may have really hurt you. They may have surprised you, shocked you, embarrassed you, or made you angry, or sad— made you cry a lot. But it is time to use the power of forgiveness **for** forgiveness to improve your life.

How Most Curses Work

Whatever was done to you, don't you keep doing it to yourself. Unforgiveness is sin and any sin is a trap. It's a curse, and most curses work something like this:

There is an ambush or a surprise--, something that you don't see coming. It's occultic, which means *hidden*, so outside of the Spirit of God there is no way to see it coming. Whatever is done to you sends you into survival mode. It's shocking, it's painful, it's disappointing–, it is traumatic. Survival mode starts and your body releases all the bad hormones that we've talked about.

This starts you out on a path that unless you are aware of it in time and seek to *spiritually* reverse it, you may not easily find your way back. When you see a medical doctor, they can't find anything wrong with you, but you may get prescriptions. Those prescriptions usually dull your symptoms. The root cause persists, so over time the problem becomes worse.

Curses start you out on some path--, a negative, evil, ungodly path and then you end up doing the rest of the damage to yourself, yourself. This especially works if you keep thinking about the problem or talking about it all day long. It becomes a self-fulfilling prophecy because faith comes by hearing, and you keep saying it. Then you start to walk along that path, because you're telling yourself to do it without being aware that that's what you're doing.

That's bad enough but seeking an ungodly person for "help" will make this even worse because now you are *all in*, all evil. Pray without ceasing, an ungodly person could be masquerading as anyone, even a pastor.

You have to pray and stay prayed up. Sin not. Holding on to bitterness can affect all parts of your life and even your physical body. It can affect your metabolism, immune system, organ functions, and can lead to physical disease, and death.

Don't let it get into your heart, into your memory, or your physical body. Most importantly, stop rehearsing it. Stop escalating it. Stop talking about it. Stop telling people about it.

It's over. It's done. It hurt. It was horrible. But you give it power when you keep talking about it. Stop talking about it and giving it **more** power.

You may need to talk to a real pastor or a trusted friend, a parent or a counselor. After that **only** talk to God about it. Putting it out in the airwaves, repeating it makes you hurt all brand new every day, giving it attention and worry gives it more power and more power over you.

Until you are fully healed from it, don't talk about it anymore. When you can talk about it with no emotional, mental or body response, *then* you're ready to tell it. When you put God at the focus, and how He brought you *through, n*ow you have a testimony. Now you have joy. Instead of hurt, you have relief. Instead of ashes, you have beauty. Now you have a **testimony**. Now shout that from the mountain tops. Run and tell that. Just run and tell it.

Inflammation

Anger, unforgiveness and bitterness are each used by the devil to steal, kill and destroy. Yes, these three that we call emotions are really evil *spirits* that can cause diseases and make people sick and terminally ill. Inflammation is the starter of most diseases. Like sour dough bread starter, yeast, or kombucha, inflammation is a *starter* that is used over and over. Anger, unforgiveness, and bitterness are each *starters* that the devil uses over and again to steal from you by repelling peace and wealth from you. They also make people sick by starting a cascade of symptoms that can both start and feed inflammation. This is how they are devil weapons.

Some of the medical causes for chronic inflammation are autoimmune diseases, exposure to toxins, pollutions, and certain chemicals. When acute inflammation lasts a long time, it is called chronic. A poor diet and malabsorption from the gut can cause inflammation, things such as fatty liver disease.

Spiritual issues that you participate in yourself, or evil that is sent your way can bring on *survival mode* and start this negative sequence of events. Spiritual and emotional stressors, and choices, such as unforgiveness can lead to malabsorption in the GI tract which can lead to inflammation.

Women's disorders such as endometriosis, or endocrine disorders in anyone, such as diabetes can set off chronic inflammation in the body. Inflammatory bowel disease, asthma, rheumatoid arthritis, and obesity can be the result with inflammation as their starter.

Inflammation can accelerate aging, leading to achy joints, stiffness, dull skin. It zaps your pretty (or handsomeness) and that's not good. Worry becomes another huge stressor as you wonder what's wrong with you and why can't the doctors fix it?

Stay prayed up. Decree and declare. The power of prayer will pull you out of survival mode and has amazing healing benefits to the body. When we proclaim things in the Name of Jesus, we will not walk into the devil's traps; we will not fall for his tactics and:

- We improve in health.
- We age gracefully,
- We will look beautiful, (handsome)
- We will be healthy,
- We function as God intended so we can reach destiny.
- We will be the person that God intended us to be from the beginning when He created us.

Senior Moments

Have you ever noticed that people, when they get a little older, might become scatterbrained, or they have what they call senior moments? Everybody thinks that's a natural part of aging. It is not. Inflammation is probably the cause of it. Of all the damage that inflammation probably does, it does the most to the brain.

So that's something we have to address as we look at inflammation, and as we age gracefully, and stay healthy.

To help heal leaky gut, sip on or cook with bone broth, it's tasty and good for you. Be sure to do the spiritual work, the cause of diseases is spiritual. Even if it's in your bloodline, it started at some spiritual crossroads with one of your ancestors and stayed in the family. Be aware. Be wise. Pray about it. Ask God. He'll show you.

Try to have an alkaline diet. Even make sure the water you drink is not acidic. Fight the devil in the natural too, eat more veggies. Whole plants contain anti-inflammatory nutrients. Use antioxidants because they help delay or repair some of the damage that's been done in your cells. Get Omega 3, 7 and also 9's.

Eat less red meat--, sorry men, and cut out the processed stuff. Stay away from and limit processed sugars, sugary cereals and drinks. Deep fried food, white starches, pastries and most desserts are all pro inflammatory.

Pray.

Spiritual Things Can Make A Person Sick

Spiritual things can make a person sick. The devil's desire is to distract, derail you, destroy you. Don't fall for his tactics.

Jesus has given us power. Like Jesus, we have the *power to forgive*. Because we have that power none of us should be too weak to forgive. Not weak of character, willpower, or ability. None of us should be too weak to forgive. Toughen it up and step to the person who may have insulted, offended or hurt you, and *forgive* them. It takes strength. It takes determination. It takes willpower. It takes love. It takes power, and Love is a power.

If you don't have love for anybody else in the scenario, have love for God because God says, **Do not let the sun go down on your wrath, on your anger.**

God does not let the sun go down on His wrath to us. I know that because the Word says **every morning there are new mercies**. Can't you be more like God, every morning, showing new mercies, even for the saints that have crossed or offended you?

In that Scripture we are also supposed to be kind to one another, forgiving one another. And we should be kind enough to give *agape* love to the person, even the person who may have hurt you.

Jesus did; He died on the Cross, forgiving all humans.

Think about it, an entire downward spiral or down cascade of symptoms, diseases and physical pain may have started with you deciding that you would never forgive *who*? _____ (Fill in the blank) Was it worth it? Don't let unforgiveness be the ***starter***.

Even if this disease that may have resulted from you not forgiving and then moving into anger, moving into resentment, moving into bitterness and chronic bitterness, and you're not willing to be reconciled back together, or at least bury the hatchet as they say. Even if you ended up with some horrible symptoms, syndrome, disorder, or disease that may have even put you at death's door, **was it worth it?**

No. It's never worth it, and it never will be.

Think back; you may have made a childhood vow, but as a teenager, a young adult or even later found that something bad happened to you. The general, *if something bad happened to me* vow that too many kids make when they hate their parents' discipline can be a *starter*.

You were a child then, and unsaved, but have you repented of that oath, wish or vow? Maybe that was the **starter** of *this* disease, this disorder, struggle, problem that has most recently happened to you. Maybe it was the start of the forming of this weapon that is being used against you now. When you as a child, in ignorance contracted with the devil. Maybe this just happened in *very slow motion*, depending on your age.

This could be a weapon that **you** helped form. Renounce and Repent! Be sure to cancel all childhood vows. Forgive others. Stay prayed up and stay healthy.

Benediction

May the Lord Jesus Christ cover you, and may He give you the strength to forgive everyone who's ever offended you, ever hurt you, ever disappointed you, ever embarrassed you. Ever made you sad. Ever made you cry.

May He give you the power. May you use that power to forgive them so **you** can be made whole – restored immediately from survival mode and its flow of negative, emotional, spiritual, somatic and soulish events, and not be subject to bitterness, the root of bitterness, or any of the stress hormones or any of the bodily symptoms, the somatic symptoms that come from being in chronic stress and survival mode.

May the Lord bless you and keep you, in Jesus' Name.

Amen.

Dear Reader

Thank you so much for acquiring and reading this book. I pray that it has given your practical and spiritual information to make your life even better than it is.

This book is a companion to the Soul Prosperity books that I've written, also for your edification.

Grace to you,

Dr. Marlene Miles

Christian books by this author

AK: The Adventures of the Agape Kid

AMONG SOME THIEVES

Ancestral Powers

Astral Projected Spirit Spouse, DIE!
https://a.co/d/6iTJI4K

Barrenness (Prayers Against) https://a.co/d/agjvhlR

& Barrenness 2 Fruit of the Womb
https://a.co/d/2Wguyhw

Blindsided: *Has the Old Man Bewitched You?*

https://a.co/d/5O2fLLR

Churchzilla, The Wanna-Be, Supposed-to-be Bride of Christ

Demonic Cobwebs (Prayers Against)
https://a.co/d/73ZQfv7   https://a.co/d/3Ayjy2J

Demons Hate Questions (mini book)

Devil Loves Trauma (The)

Devil Weapons: Unforgiveness, Bitterness,…

Dream Defilement https://a.co/d/1pLX6hY

Don't Refuse Me, Lord (4 book series)

Every Evil Bird https://a.co/d/csfbY8F

Evil Touch https://a.co/d/9fuRygQ

Fantasy Spirit Spouse

FAT Demons (The): *Breaking Demonic Curses*

The Fold (4 book series)

- The Fold (Book 1)
- Name Your Seed (Book 2)
- The Poor Attitudes of Money (3)
- Do Not Orphan Your Seed

got HEALING? Verses for Life

got LOVE? Verses for Life

got HOPE? Verses for Life

got money?

How to Dental Assist

How to Dental Assit2: Be Productive, Not Wasteful

Let Me Have A Dollar's Worth

Living for the NOW of God

Lose My Location https://a.co/d/crD6mV9

Man Safari, *The*

Marriage Ed. Rules of Engagement & Marriage

Made Perfect in Love

Motherboard (The) - soul prosperity series

Pass Over Me, My House (Let My People Go) Prayer book https://a.co/d/bo8FC4I

Plantation Souls

Power Money: Nine Times the Tithe

The Power of Wealth *(forthcoming)*

Rules of Engagement & Marriage

Seasons of Grief

Seasons of Waiting https://a.co/d/3Uxr5lC

Seasons of War

Sift You Like Wheat

Soul Prosperity Series https://a.co/d/bz2M42q

https://a.co/d/5p8YvCN

Souls in Captivity, Soul Prosperity series, Book 2

The Spirit of Poverty

Spirits of Death & the Grave, PASS OVER Me & My House
https://a.co/d/bo8FC4I   (see above, Pass Over)

This Is NOT That: How to Keep Demons from Coming at You

Throne of Grace: Courtroom Prayer

Time Is of the Essence

Too Many Wives: *Why You Have Lady Problems*

Tormenting Spirits   https://a.co/d/dAogEJf

Triangular Power *(series)*

- Powers Above
- SUNBLOCK
- Do Not Swear by the Moon
- STARSTRUCK

Uncontested Doom

Upgrade: How to Get Out of Survival Mode

- Toxic Souls (Book 2 of series)
- Legacy (Book 3 of series)

Warfare Prayer Against Beauty Curses

Warfare Prayer Against Poverty

What Have You to Declare?

When the Devourer is Rebuked

When You See Blood

The Wilderness Romance *(series)* This is not a romance series. This is how to avoid meeting/dating/marrying a person who is a Wilderness man or Wilderness woman.

The series is about how to handle yourself if you are in such a marriage. Know the signs so you don't get caught up!

- *The Social Wilderness*
- *The Sexual Wilderness*
- *The Spiritual Wilderness*

Other Series:

The Fold (a series on Godly finances)
https://a.co/d/4hz3unj

Thieves of Darkness series

Triangular Powers https://a.co/d/aUCjAWC

What are the Triangular Powers and why are they so dangerous?

Upgrade (series) *How to Get Out of Survival Mode* https://a.co/d/aTERhXO